MW01294417

Kevin Love: The Inspiring Story of One of Basketball's Dominant Power Forwards

An Unauthorized Biography

By: Clayton Geoffreys

Table of Contents

Foreword

Few stories brought as much attention in the summer of 2014 than LeBron James' return to the Cleveland Cavaliers. It was called a homecoming, and rightfully so as the King had left his hometown team four years before. Yet, one story quickly emerged after LeBron announced his homecoming and that story was of Kevin Love. While he spent the last six years playing for the Minnesota Timberwolves, it has long been speculated that Love would be on the move in the summer of 2014. Ultimately as the summer concluded, it became official and Kevin Love joined the Cleveland Cavaliers as part of a blockbuster trade involving one of the most anticipated upcoming players: Andrew Wiggins. Love's impact in Minnesota was often overlooked due to his lack of a strong supporting cast; however, Love was dominant and truly was none other than the superstar for Minnesota. Kevin Love's ascent as a star was not easy, as you will learn in this book. Thank you for purchasing *Kevin Love:*

The Inspiring Story of One of Basketball's Dominant Power Forwards. In this unauthorized biography, we will learn Kevin Love's incredible life story and impact on the game of basketball. Hope you enjoy and if you do, please do not forget to leave a review!

Also, check out my website at claytongeoffreys.com to join my exclusive list where I let you know about my latest books. To thank you for your purchase, you can go to my site to download a free copy of *33 Life Lessons: Success Principles, Career Advice & Habits of Successful People*. In the book, you'll learn from some of the greatest thought leaders of different industries on what it takes to become successful and how to live a great life.

Cheers,

Clayton Geoffreys

Visit me at www.claytongeoffreys.com

Introduction

In basketball, the effect of a superstar is gigantic compared to in other sports. In baseball, an elite hitter will get only about as many chances as his teammates, and his defense only matters if the ball is hit towards him. In football, while the impact of a quarterback might be comparable to a star, the fact that football players only play offense or defense limits their capabilities. Time and time again in NBA history, we have seen great superstars lead mediocre supporting teams to high regular season win totals and playoff success. Kobe Bryant won 45 games in 2006 with an incredibly weak Lakers supporting roster. Tim Duncan earned a championship in 2003 even though his best playoff teammates were David Robinson with one foot in the grave as well as various other players who were too young to reach their ultimate potential. LeBron James dragged the 2007 Cavaliers to the NBA Finals. Unlike the other leagues, NBA stars have shown that they are fully capable of creating great results almost entirely by themselves as just one superstar. One superstar is nearly all

4

that's needed in the NBA game for a team to turn around its fortunes.

If this is true, then what are we to make of Kevin Love? The newest member of the Cleveland Cavaliers spent the first six years of his career as the star for the Minnesota Timberwolves. The Timberwolves never won more than 40 games during Love's tenure. They routinely struggled during the close games where superstars are supposed to take over. They were never a top 10 defensive team, which is particularly concerning given that superstar big men can make a huge difference on that end. It is true that Kevin Love put up staggering numbers, but how much impact did he create if the Wolves never made the playoffs? Is Love a superstar who was cursed to play with mediocre talent in Minnesota and now will make Cleveland the most dangerous team in the league? Or is he an overrated player who looked out for his numbers above the team's, never won anything in the NBA, and will not help the Cavaliers as much as people expect?

When Love was playing in Minnesota, there was no doubt in anyone's mind that he was a legitimate superstar player.

His first year didn't start out with a bang, but he developed into one of the best, if not the best, rebounders in the whole league. Kevin Love has routinely figured in double-digit rebounding since his second year in the league, and he's even led the NBA in rebounding for one season when he was a walking 20-20 on scoring and on rebounding. In that season, he even went for a rare game of over 30 points and 30 rebounds. That's how much of a monster Love was in his days as a Timberwolf.

Since his breakout third season in the NBA, Kevin Love has been a perennial All-Star and has consistently been in the conversation of best power forwards or even best big men in the NBA. How could he not be? Kevin Love could rebound at the highest rate possible. We know that. He could score inside and in the post as well as any other power forward. But what made him better than other big men was the fact that he could shoot the three-pointer at a level that could rival shooting guards. Aside from his shooting touch, Kevin Love has always been a terrific passer for a big man. No other power forward in the NBA could hit a touchdown pass as good as Love can. That's how talented of a player Love is. That's why he's always been one of the most sought-after names in the NBA.

As good of a player as he is, Kevin was not perfect. He had a few chinks in his armor. While Kevin Love's game has flaws, he is still one of the best players in the NBA. In his years with the Timberwolves, the staggering incompetence of Minnesota's management meant that Love got players that were good or complemented his skill sets. Inexperienced and incompetent general manager David Kahn routinely screwed up in the draft and free agency. Love also played in a brutal Western Conference where teams routinely had to win 45 games or more to make the playoffs. Had he played in the weaker Eastern Conference, it is very likely that he would have won more games, made the playoffs, and thus earned a different reputation.

Because of Love's inability to win in Minnesota despite numbers that could rival all-time greats, he's faced criticisms that he might not be the kind of superstar that could bring a team to greatness all the way out from limbo. Some may even wonder if he was a superstar to begin with. Kevin might have had those impressive numbers only because there were no other reliable players on the Timberwolves' roster. Maybe Love was a guy who could get 20 rebounds because everybody was missing shots and nobody else could rebound. Maybe he could put up 30 points on the board because nobody else could. Maybe he just simply stood out because he was the biggest fish in a small pond. Those were the kind of criticisms he was facing.

Of course, Love's chance to answer the critics is finally here. Will he be able to help LeBron James give the city of Cleveland their first sports championship in over 50 years this upcoming season? Will he be continuing a legacy of winning which followed him until he joined the Timberwolves? Or will he be left unheralded in a team full of talent? Those questions remain unanswered as Kevin Love continues his NBA journey towards a much more meaningful and successful career.

Chapter 1: Childhood and Early Life

Kevin Wesley Love was born on September 7, 1988 to Karen and Stan Love in Santa Monica, California. Stan had played for the NBA and ABA during the early 1970s. His playing career was not particularly impressive; even though he had been selected 9th in the 1971 NBA Draft by the Baltimore Bullets, he played just four seasons with the Bullets and Los Angeles Lakers before retiring in 1975. He averaged 6.6 points and 3.9 rebounds in those four years. Kevin Love would score more points in his 2013-14 season than Stan did in his entire professional basketball career.

However, even though Stan had not played basketball for over a decade by the time his second son was born, he taught Kevin everything that he could about the sport. You can even go on to say that Stan's genes played a significant role in making Kevin as good of a player as he is right now. He gave Kevin his middle name after NBA Hall of Fame player Westley "Wes" Unseld, who Love would eventually mirror as an NBA superstar. As an infant, Love held basketballs in his crib and stroller. At the age of 5, he declared to a family friend that he wanted to become an

NBA player when he grew up. These were not the childish words thrown about so casually in one's youth. Love was committed to basketball, and his willingness to practice became apparent from a young age.

In the town of Lake Oswego, Oregon where he grew up, Love worked on his shooting, free throws, and other aspects of basketball. In one drill, Stan and Kevin would get in a car. Stan would drive the vehicle at about 10 mph, and Love had to dribble a basketball outside of the car window. Love also showed his dedication to the sport outside of practice. While other children watched Sesame Street or cartoons, Love watched videos of NBA greats like Hakeem Olajuwon, Larry Bird, and Michael Jordan. He even watched videos on how to improve his post play and what drills were best to practice! Out of all the stars he watched, Love particularly liked Wes Unseld and Larry Bird. When it came to current stars, Love respected Elton Brand, who was an MVP candidate with the Los Angeles Clippers in 2006.

Stan helped his son improve with basketball, but he was a true father as well. He was not an overbearing parent who forced Kevin into basketball as a way of making up for his short professional basketball career. When Kevin's older brother Collin moved away from basketball to pursue other interests, Stan had no objections. Stan is also the younger brother of the founder of the rock band The Beach Boys, so he showed his three children Collin, Kevin, and youngest daughter Emily a great deal about music. While Stan made sure to raise all three of his kids with love, he was also more than happy to pound on Kevin's door early in the morning to make sure that his son got to morning basketball workouts on time. Kevin has joked that his father is "insane" and "eccentric" in interviews, but he has thanked him for the positive influence he had on his eventual basketball career.

Chapter 2: High School Years

In 2003, Kevin Love entered the local high school, Lake Oswego High School. Lake Oswego was not a renowned basketball school, nor did it possess any famous basketball alumni before Kevin Love. The minute Love stepped onto the court, his talent became apparent to Coach Mark Shoff. Love had always been large throughout his childhood. In middle school, he had to sit at a different desk and table that were specially designed to accommodate his height. Now at well over 6 feet, Love had also worked on his shooting and ball handling. From the very beginning, his outlet passes were on point, just like they would be in the NBA. Shoff decided instantly to place Love on the varsity team despite his freshman status and use him as a center.

The decision turned out to be correct. In Love's freshman year, Lake Oswego improved to a 19-9 record for the season. They finished third in the local Three Rivers League and qualified for the Oregon School Activities Association tournament. Love averaged 13 points as a freshman. Over the summer, he continued to show his work ethic and dedication towards improving his game. Even when it rained as it so often does in Oregon, Love practiced outside with the rain drops splashing onto his body.

It was Love's sophomore year when he began to show that he was not just another varsity player. In a precursor to his staggering NBA numbers, Love averaged 25 points, 15 rebounds, and four assists that season. These numbers translated to wins, and Lake Oswego improved to a 21-8 record that year and made it all to the way to the state championship game. Love earned the Oregon Player of the Year as a sophomore. In his junior year, he improved again to average 28 points, 16 rebounds, and four assists. Lake Oswego now finished as the number two team in Oregon with a 26-3 record. Against number one South Menford led by future NBA player Kyle Singler, the Lake Oswego Lakers prevailed 59-57 to win their first state championship. Kevin Love had 24 points and ten rebounds in that game. He was once again named Oregon Player of the Year.

At this point, Love was not just one of the top prospects in Oregon, but in the United States. In Amateur Athletic Union (AAU) basketball, Love showed off his dominance by joining the Southern California All-Stars in 2006 alongside future NBA player Brandon Jennings. The All-Stars played 47 games in their summer circuit and won all 47. Today, they are remembered as one of the greatest AAU teams to have ever existed. Thanks to Love's success both at the high school and AAU levels, he was ranked as one of the top prospects in the country behind high school phenomenon O.J. Mayo. The citizens of Lake Oswego and Oregon expected that Kevin would join the University of Oregon after he graduated from high school. Stan Love had been a star for Oregon for four years before he entered the NBA, so why should the son not follow the father?

One man had very different plans. UCLA Coach Ben Howland had been following Kevin Love since Love was in eighth grade. He hung around the Lake Oswego campus so often that Coach Shoff joked that he thought Howland "was a member of the faculty." Howland offered Love the chance to come to California and play with other local stars like Arron Afflalo and Jordan Farmar. Stan Love was also interested in seeing his son play for UCLA. He hoped to play for the school back in his playing days, but had to settle for Oregon. Love considered joining Oregon and playing alongside many of his high school friends. He considered heading to North Carolina and following in the footsteps of all-time greats like Jordan. Nevertheless, in 2006, right before Love began his senior year, he announced that he would be joining UCLA.

Local fans were upset about this decision, but the fact was that Love had never been on the best terms with Lake Oswego. Kevin noted that while O.J. Mayo could have thousands of fans and elite NBA players like LeBron and Carmelo come to watch his games, Lake Oswego High School could not even fill up their local arena outside of the high school playoffs. In his senior year, Love improved once again and averaged 34 points, 17 rebounds, and four assists. In a game against Putnam High School, which was played on January 12, 2007, Love intercepted the ball from the opposing point guard, raced down the court, and shattered the backboard with his dunk! Love was nominated the Oregon Player of the Year for the third straight year, the most in the state's history. He was also nominated for the Gatorade National Male Athlete of the Year, an All-American First Team player, and the Naismith Prep Player of the Year, among other awards. Despite these accomplishments, Lake Oswego High School did not name Love their athlete of the year. Instead, they gave it to a golf player. Love would later say to Sports Illustrated that he believed the people of Lake Oswego "never really respected me."

On the basketball court, Love led Lake Oswego a 27-2 record and the state championship finals, where they once again matched up against South Menford. Lake Oswego's team was weaker compared to the previous year. Love scored 37 points in the game, including 24 straight at one point. Nevertheless, South Menford prevailed 58-54, and Love's high school career was over. Even though his final game was a defeat, he had a great deal to be proud of. In his four years with Lake Oswego, Kevin Love had averaged around 26 points and 15 rebounds. He finished as the leading scorer in Oregon history with 2,682 total points and grabbed the record for most points in an Oregon high school game at that time with 50.

Off the basketball court, Love initially cut classes and sat in the back cracking jokes in his early years. Math teacher Scott Buchannan had a different idea. He forced Love to sit at the front and learn. He would remind Love of the importance of education and tell him that he had a great opportunity to be a role model for others in the community. It was a lesson that Love would take to heart in the future, and he continues to stay in touch with Buchannan to this day.

Chapter 3: College Years at UCLA

When Kevin Love entered UCLA, it was widely understood both by the media as well as Coach Howland that he would be there for at most two years. If the NBA had not banned the practice of high school players joining the NBA directly in 2006, it is possible that Love may have taken the leap straight to the NBA. Regardless, no one doubted that when Love entered the NBA, he would be one of the top draft picks in his year.

Still, that did not mean Kevin Love had nothing to learn from UCLA, and he knew that. One of the first things Love did when he arrived at the campus was contact the school's former legendary coach, John Wooden. Most UCLA players did not do that, but Love continually called Wooden at least once a month to ask him about the work ethic of past UCLA greats like Bill Walton and Kareem Abdul-Jabbar, Wooden's famed Pyramid of Success, and endless stories of Wooden's coaching days. Like most incoming college freshman, Love had a period where he struggled to adjust to the greater physicality of college basketball as well as the greater demands on the defensive end. But after a few preseason games, Love finally managed to figure things out. On November 9, 2007, Love made his college basketball debut against Portland State. In his very first game, he started at center, scored 22 points on just eight shots, and grabbed 13 rebounds.

From there, the UCLA Bruins continued to dominate the league. Love became the best player on the team, but he was not alone. Junior point guard Darren Collison had been reliable for the Bruins over the years, but his injury at the beginning of the season permitted an athletic but inconsistent player named Russell Westbrook to get his chance to shine. Luc Richard Mbah a Moute also provided veteran leadership. Under Coach Howland, the UCLA Bruins won 16 of their first 17 games. On January 12, 2008, Love scored a season-high 27 points against Washington State.

About two weeks later, the Bruins played at the University of Oregon, the school that Love was supposed to have joined in the mind of its fans. Oregon's reception was shockingly brutal. Fans somehow managed to get ahold of Love's cellphone number before the game and sent him over 30 death threats regarding him and his family. Homophobic insults were spewed, the Love family was pelted with popcorn cartons, and they had to get security to watch their son play a basketball game. Afterward, Stan Love, the former Oregon star, declared that he would never return to the school. Love responded not by throwing insults back or attacking the fans, but by scoring 26 points and 18 rebounds to lead UCLA to the 80-75 victory. When Oregon came to UCLA about a month later, UCLA prevailed again by a score of 75-65. In that game, Love had 15 points and 11 rebounds. It is possible that the crowd's boos and jeers only inspired him.

At the end of the regular season, the UCLA Bruins finished with a 28-3 record. They won the Pac-10 tournament and finished with the first seed in the West group of the NCAA tournament. Love and Darren Collison led UCLA throughout the first rounds of the NCAA tournament, and they reached the Final Four where they faced off against Derrick Rose and Chris Douglas-Roberts. Unfortunately, Memphis's tough defense completely stifled not just Love, but all of the UCLA players except Westbrook. Love scored 12 points on 4-11 shooting while Rose and Douglas-Roberts had 25 and 28 points respectively. Memphis prevailed over the Bruins 78-63, and UCLA's season was over. Over the course of his one NCAA season, Love averaged 17.5 points on 56% shooting and 10.6 rebounds. He also shot around 35% from 3-point range.

Chapter 4: Kevin's NBA Career

Getting Drafted

About two weeks after the loss to Memphis, Love announced that he would forgo the final three years of his college eligibility and enter the NBA Draft. Draft scouts were excited to analyze Love's strengths and weaknesses. As a center in college, Kevin was a guy who stood about 6'9" entering the 2008 NBA Draft. However, he was young at that time. He would grow to about 6'10" in his time as a professional. For a young guy out of college, Love was also a big body. He weighed about 255 pounds. While most of that wasn't muscle, it was clear that Kevin had the body to get physical with the big men in the NBA. Though his arms weren't really long, they were longer than most people expected. That's what allowed him to play the center spot for UCLA despite his apparent lack of height. However, his wingspan wasn't needed because Love's physicality and large body were all he needed to bully taller players in the paint.

Love was praised for his strong basketball IQ, passing game, and post play. Because of those skills, he was often compared to Wes Unseld, one of his longtime idols. Kevin was described as a player who played with a lot of physicality. With a big body like his, it wouldn't be difficult for Kevin to bang with big men inside the paint. Not only was he a good player down at the low post, his fundamentals at getting to that position were almost flawless. Kevin knew how to use his body to pin his defenders down. And with his large hands, Kevin Love could easily catch inside passes from his teammates. Once he got his position and the ball from his teammates, there was almost no stopping him from scoring, especially with how soft his touch was from the inside.

While low post games are staple skills for a man as big as Kevin, what made him a real prospect were the other parts of his game. Kevin Love was always a gifted passer, even back in his younger days. Not a lot of big men have that skill. When post players get the ball, all they could think of is scoring. But love was different. He had a good sense about the game and used his ability to make passes from the post to find open teammates out on the perimeter. And when he got the rebound, all you had to do as a guard was to keep running down the floor because there was always a good chance that Kevin Love could find you with his quick outlet passes. Even at the collegiate level, his passing abilities were already better than any other big men in the NBA.

Other than his passing skills, Love was a gifted shooter for a big man. He routinely shot the college three-pointer at a respectable percentage. It wouldn't take a long time for him to adjust to the distance of the NBA three-pointer. His three-point shot wasn't the only thing that made him a dangerous scorer. Love could also score from the perimeter. When he catches the ball between the paint and the three-point line, he seems comfortable doing things that guards do. He would use jab steps and fakes to keep his defenders off-balanced for easy drives at the basket. If given enough space to shoot, he will put the ball in the hoop via face-up jumpers or dribble pull-ups.

With all of Kevin Love's offensive skills highlighted, what made him an even better prospect was his rebounding.

Love has a very high basketball IQ for a big man. Such a high IQ for the game helps players understand when to make passes or when to cut. Love does all of that in addition to using his basketball smarts to know when and where to position for rebounding. Using his sense for the game, Kevin has a nose for the ball in rebounding situations. And with his big body, he could easily get good positions to box out his opponents for rebounds. His timing and instincts were simply impeccable when going up for rebounds. And even for a pudgy player, Kevin Love could jump higher than most people thought. That's why he was a walking double-double in his lone year with UCLA.

On the other hand, there were concerns about his defense, conditioning, and speed. Defensively, he was merely about 6'9" entering the NBA. Though he had longer arms than most people would expect, they weren't long enough to cover what he lacked in height. That's why he couldn't block a lot of shots in college. His lack of lateral movement was also a defensive liability, especially on switches and when matched up against quicker opponents.

Love was also often winded as a player. That was an apparent evidence of his lack of conditioning. The biggest culprit of that was all the pudgy weight he'd been carrying. He might have been 255 pounds, but most of that wasn't muscle. He had a lot of body fat slowing him down as a player. While his fat and weight helped him overpower his lankier defenders in the amateur stages, Love can't get away with that in the NBA, especially because the other big men were built solidly and more muscular. In college, you would often see him as the last player up or down the court because of his lack of stamina. And, because Love hustled a lot on rebounding, he quickly got drained of his energy.

Because of his weight and conditioning, Kevin Love was also very slow. His legs often kept him anchored on the floor as he could rarely jump high or even run at his full speed. Though he could move quickly, his full sprint was so slow that he could rarely figure himself into transition plays. If there was something Love needed to work on first as an NBA player, it would have to be his conditioning. He needed to lose a lot of weight and pack in a lot of beef to take away all of his shortcomings as a player.

Despite a lot of weaknesses, most NBA mock drafts had him going at number 5 to the Memphis Grizzlies, though some had him as high as 4 and some as low as 9. That was because he was still one of the most talented players on the offensive end and rebounding. Love was still a player you could count on to develop into an All-Star. Hence, on June 26, 2008, Love was indeed selected by the Memphis Grizzlies with the fifth pick, one behind his college teammate Russell Westbrook. Love excitedly donned a Memphis hat and shook hands with NBA Commissioner David Stern. He had finally arrived in the NBA.

However, he would not be with Memphis as it turned out. Shortly afterward, the Grizzlies traded Love to the Minnesota Timberwolves for O.J. Mayo. Minnesota General Manager Kevin McHale, one of the greatest post players in NBA history as a Boston Celtic, saw himself in Kevin Love. The Timberwolves had drafted Mayo with the third pick to gain additional assets like sharpshooter Mike Miller and shed some bad contracts all while obtaining the player that they wanted. Love was undoubtedly excited to play under someone as respected as McHale.

Rookie Season

Unfortunately, the Minnesota Timberwolves were a disaster in 2008. They had last made the playoffs back in 2004 when Kevin Garnett and Sam Cassell had led the team to the Western Conference Finals. Since then, the Wolves had been so terrible that even Garnett had proven unable to drag them back to the playoffs. After two years of failure, they traded for what was at the time viewed as a bonanza of picks and players with high potential, including skilled center Al Jefferson and wing player Gerald Green. However, Minnesota struggled without Garnett and won only 22 games in the 2007-08 season. While the Timberwolves believed that Love would need some time to develop into a true NBA star, they were confident that they could turn it around in his rookie season behind Jefferson.

It turned out not to be the case. The Timberwolves had won just four of their first 19 games before they decided to fire Coach Randy Wittman. Love made his debut coming off the bench for 12 points and nine rebounds in just 18 minutes in a win against the Sacramento Kings. Coach Wittman placed Love in the starting lineup by the fifth game of the season, but Love struggled in that role and was removed. In his first game as a starter, Love scored 20 points on 6 out of 7 shooting from the floor. He also had eight rebounds in 30 minutes of action. But his team lost that game by 12. In the next three games as a starter, he would combine for merely 16 points on 5 out of 22 shooting. All three games were losses. It was clear that he was not yet ready for that role.

When Kevin McHale stepped down from his General Manager position to take Wittman's place as coach, he continued to keep Love on the bench. Love worked under McHale to improve his post play and handle the physicality of the NBA. He developed a great respect for the Celtics legend and tried to retain everything that McHale taught him. Under McHale, he was the first big man off the bench as he backed up Al Jefferson and Craig Smith.

On November 29, 2008, Kevin Love had his first double-double in his NBA career. He had 18 points and 12 rebounds, which included six on the offensive end, in 28 minutes off the bench in a losing effort to the Denver Nuggets. A few days later, he had 16 points and 12 rebounds in a loss to the Orlando Magic. He had eight offensive boards in that game. From December 6 all the way to 15, Kevin Love had six consecutive games of double-digit rebounding. He first had 13 points and 15 boards in a sorry loss to the LA Clippers. He then went on to collect eight offensive rebounds for a total of 15 boards against the Utah Jazz. He would have 14, 10, 10, and 15 rebounds in the next four games. All six of those games were losses as the Wolves found themselves on a 13-game streak. However, Love was still able to display how good of a rebounder he is despite some apparent difficulties on the offensive end.

On January 3, 2009, Kevin Love had 18 points and 12 rebounds in just 21 minutes of action as he helped his team get a win against the Chicago Bulls. It was a rarity for Love to play well in wins in his rookie season. He then had 16 points and 15 rebounds in just 23 minutes on the floor as his team walloped the Oklahoma City Thunder by 42 points. He would then have 13 points and 14 boards in a narrow win in Phoenix. It seemed like everything was going well for Love as he then had 19 points and 15 boards in a win against the Bulls.

From January 20 to 30, Love found himself scoring in double digits in six straight outings. He had two double-figure rebounding games in that streak. He would then rebound in double figures in five of next six games before the All-Star break. To the surprise of a lot of NBA spectators, Kevin Love was not selected to participate in the All-Star Rookie Challenge despite being the best rebounding rookie of the season.

For a short time under McHale, the Wolves seemed to be turning things around and went 10-4 at one point. However, Jefferson tore his ACL in February. This ended any hope of Minnesota making any run to the playoffs, so they focused their effort during the second half of the season on developing talent like Love. Like many rookies, Love remained inconsistent throughout his first season. Even though he had been a good 3-point shooter in college, he hit only two 3-pointers in his first NBA season. Despite

Kevin McHale's coaching, Love struggled in the post against the NBA's tougher and more athletic defenders. He also had problems keeping up with faster forwards on the defensive end.

Despite these problems, Love showed flashes of a potential NBA star. His biggest positive asset was his rebounding ability. Even though Love lacked the great leaping ability which most elite rebounders possess, he had an excellent sense of timing which enabled him to get into position both on the offensive and defensive end. His rebounding numbers per minute were already among the league's best and beat other great big men like Tim Duncan and Tyson Chandler. Love's ability to grab the offensive rebound also gave him easier chances to score, and he finally became a consistent double-digit scorer in the second half of the 2008-09 regular season.

Since Jefferson's injury, Love stepped up to take the starting center spot. It was then and there when he started to show flashes of his future superstar self as he consistently figured in double digits in both scoring and rebounding. On February 25, he would have a then career high of 24 points while also grabbing 15 rebounds, which included eight offensive ones, in a loss to the Utah Jazz. Love played 36 minutes that game as he went 10 out of 12 from the floor. About a week later, he would have 18 markers and 14 boards in a big loss to the Golden State Warriors. In the game after that, he had identical numbers in a loss to the Lakers.

On March 14, Love went for 22 points on 9 out of 17 shooting against the Charlotte Bobcats in a win. In his next game, he grabbed had 17 points and 19 big rebounds even as he was matched up against Tim Duncan, one of the all-time great power forwards the league has ever seen. The Wolves would only lose by 7 points that game as Love dominated the boards. In the following night, Kevin went for 23 points and 11 boards in a narrow loss to the Hornets. He would round up that three-game stretch with 18 points and 12 boards in a loss to the Houston Rockets on March 20. Kevin Love would score in double digits six more times as he finished a nine-game stretch of double-digit scoring. At the end of that stretch, he had 23 points and 12 rebounds in a blowout loss to the Dallas Mavericks.

As the regular season came to a close, the Minnesota Timberwolves had barely improved that season, winning just 24 games in 2008-09 as opposed to 22 the year before. Al Jefferson scored the most points on the team even though he missed 32 games with that torn ACL. Even Love was viewed as another disappointment. He averaged 11 points and nine rebounds in 25 minutes of play and made the All-Rookie Second Team. However, O.J. Mayo had scored 18.5 points in his rookie year, made the All-Rookie First Team, and had finished second in Rookie of the Year voting behind Chicago Bulls guard Derrick Rose. Sports writers and Minnesota fans were convinced that trading Love for Mayo was just another example in the long history of Minnesota's disappointing management. However, Mayo would not develop much more from his rookie, and Love's rise was just beginning.

First Double-Double Season

For the time being, things were about to get even worse for the Timberwolves. Shortly after the 2008-09 regular season ended, Minnesota decided to hire David Kahn, a sportswriter with no actual basketball roster managerial experience, as their new general manager. Kahn declared after his arrival that he believed Love's ceiling was as the fourth-best player on a championship team. During the 2009 NBA Draft, the Wolves, led by the general manager Kahn, drafted several point guards in the first round. He then traded Ty Lawson, who was the most NBA ready, to the Denver Nuggets During the offseason, Kahn selected Kurt Rambis to replace McHale as the new Minnesota coach. Rambis used to play for the Los Angeles Lakers and had been an assistant coach under Phil Jackson for almost a decade. Minnesota hoped that Rambis could teach Jackson's famous triangle offense to the young Timberwolves.

The result in the 2009-10 season was a disaster both for the Timberwolves and Kevin Love. Rambis's opinion of Love was even worse than Kahn's. He believed that Love would be best suited to the role of a sixth man, and so benched him in favor of players like Ryan Hollins and, later, draft bust Darko Milicic. Love also broke his left hand at the beginning of the season and missed the first 18 games. During that stretch, Minnesota won just twice. When Love returned, Rambis steadily decreased his minutes for most of the season. Darko grabbed a larger share of the offense to finish out the season, and David Kahn would infamously describe the center as "manna from heaven."

Despite that initial setback, Love made his 2009-10 debut on December 4, 2009 by immediately recording a double-double. He had 11 points and 11 rebounds in just 24 minutes in a loss to New Orleans. In his next game, he led the Timberwolves to a win against Utah as he posted 18 points and ten rebounds in just 26 minutes. He would then have 18 and 12 in his third and fourth games respectively. In his fifth game of the season, Love would tie his career best in rebounding by grabbing 19 boards in a loss to the Los Angeles Lakers on December 11. That was his first start of the season.

Since starting, Kevin Love racked up the numbers. He had 12 straight double-digit rebounding games since getting inserted into the starting lineup. He also had 14 consecutive double-digit scoring games, which included 11 straight double-doubles. Love had games worth mentioning in that stretch. He had 20 points, 16 rebounds, and five assists in a 16-point win against the Kings. Though it came at a 25-point loss, Love scored 15 and tied his career high of 19 rebounds versus the Atlanta Hawks. On December 30, he even had a near triple-double as he recorded 17 points, 11 rebounds, and nine assists in a loss to the Utah Jazz.

On January 6, 2010, Kevin Love had 23 points, 15 rebounds, and six dimes in a loss to the Warriors. He followed that game up by recording 18 points and 13 boards in a win versus the Indiana Pacers. On January 11, he would have another 20-10 game as he finished a loss to Denver with 20 points and 14 rebounds. After that game, Love would have six more double-digit rebounding games in the next ten outings. As the All-Star Weekend dawned, Love was selected to participate in the Rookie Challenge after being snubbed the previous season.

In his first game after the midseason break, Kevin Love had 22 points and 15 rebounds in a loss to the Detroit Pistons. At that point, Love was relegated to the bench as he lost his starting spot once again. In his first ten games since the All-Star break, Love had seven double-doubles despite coming off the bench. Despite his performances, the Minnesota Timberwolves still saw themselves losing games after games as they 14 straight outings.

On March 28, in the final game of that 14-game losing stretch, Kevin Love posted his first 20-20 game. He had 23 points and 22 rebounds in a narrow loss to the Phoenix Suns. Love was 8 out of 17 from the field and had eight offensive rebounds in that game. He would have five more double-doubles in his final eight games. At one point, he had consecutive games of 18 rebounds. He scored 17 and 12 in those games. Minnesota would lose the last seven games of the regular season and would miss the postseason once again.

Even amidst the chaos of Minnesota, Love still continued to show signs that he could break out if given consistent minutes. He led the league in rebounding per minute, grabbing 11 in less than 29 minutes of play. Love also was slowly adjusting to the longer NBA 3-point line and shot 33% from there that season. Kevin Love averaged his first double-double season, posing norms of 14 points, 11 rebounds, and 2.3 assists. With 3.8 offensive boards per game, Love was one of the best glass cleaners on the attacking end of the floor. His rebounding was always a constant, but his offense was growing as he was shooting more from the floor while maintaining the same efficiency.

Despite his improvement, he was still not on the level of a superstar. Love averaged only 28.6 minutes while starting only 22 games out of 60 that season. One could argue that he was still far from the conditioned body everyone expected from him as he could not even play more than 30 minutes per game. Plus, he was also playing in a struggling team Rambis's incompetent coaching as well as a mediocre season from the entire team meant that Minnesota only managed to win 15 games that season.

Breakout All-Star Year

During the 2010 offseason, the Timberwolves traded away Al Jefferson and picked up Michael Beasley, who had been taken two slots before Love in the 2008 NBA Draft. With Al Jefferson gone, the widespread assumption was that Love would receive more playing time during the 2010-11 season. However, while Kurt Rambis did place Love in the starting lineup, he ended up giving minutes to Beasley and journeyman power forward Anthony Tolliver. When Rambis was asked about Love's minutes, he declared that, "Kevin Love's minutes are only limited by how he plays." Given his coach's lack of faith in him, it was clear that Love would need to do something incredible to show how good he could be.

So he did just that. Kevin Love came into the 2010-11 season better conditioned. He was no longer the fat and pudgy teenager that came out of UCLA. He was better built and had shed a lot of fat while gaining muscle. He maintained his weight of about 250 pounds and he needed every bit of it when grinding against the physical big men of the NBA. With his better conditioning and stamina, Kevin Love became the team's starting power forward. Still, Rambis didn't declare Love as his best player. Kevin would have to prove that with his play throughout the season.

Kevin Love started the season with three straight double-doubles. However, those double-doubles weren't all that spectacular as he merely scored 11, 17, and 14 while grabbing 10, 16, and 13 in his first three games of the

2010-11 season. On November 2 and 3, Love went for consecutive games of scoring at least 20 points as he poured 20 on the Miami Heat and then 22 on the Orlando Magic. However, the Wolves lost both games by a total margin of 74. After those games, he would have 18 points and 12 rebounds on the Atlanta Hawks, and then 16 points and 16 boards in a big loss to the Houston Rockets. As good as Love was at that point, it wasn't enough to get him to the level of an All-Star.

On November 9, 2010, Love grabbed 24 rebounds against the defending champions, the Los Angeles Lakers, and their frontcourt duo of Pau Gasol and Lamar Odom. Kevin grabbed a then career-best 11 offensive rebounds together with 13 defensive ones as he had a virtual triple-double game. He also had 23 points on 7 out of 17 shooting in that phenomenal match. However, they lost that outing as the Timberwolves fell to a record of 1-7 to start the season.

Three days later, the Timberwolves faced off against the New York Knicks. Love did not score his first points of the game until halfway through the second quarter, and New York eventually took a 78-60 lead. But Love grabbed 15 rebounds in the third quarter, three short of the NBA record for rebounds in a quarter, and took over the scoring in the third and fourth quarters off of offensive putbacks. With two minutes left in the game, Love grabbed his 31st rebound, a Minnesota record. Two minutes later, Love hit a 3-pointer to score 31 points as well. It was the first 30-30 performance since Moses Malone back in 1982. Thanks to Love's efforts, Minnesota rallied to defeat New York 112-103. Kurt Rambis pulled Love off of the floor in the final minute. A Minnesota crowd, which had been rendered inert by years of losing, stood up and cheered their new superstar. That was the moment that signified Love's rise to the top.

After the 30-30 game, everything changed. Rambis finally gave Love the minutes he deserved and watched as Love blossomed into a real star. In the very next game against Atlanta, Love had 22 points and 17 rebounds. About two weeks later, Love finished with 32 points and 22 rebounds in an overtime game against the San Antonio Spurs. In the match after that, Kevin had 21 points and 22 rebounds in 42 minutes in a loss to the Golden State Warriors.

Since grabbing 17 rebounds on November 22 in a loss to the OKC Thunder, Kevin Love was in a 14-game streak of rebounding 14 or more rebounds. All 14 games were double-doubles. On December 8, he had another 20-20 game as he recorded 21 points and 22 in a loss to the Thunder. In the game after that, Love's monstrous numbers finally gave a win to the Timberwolves he posted 27 points and 18 boards in a win against the Detroit Pistons. He would end that streak by posting a then career-high 43 points together with 17 rebounds in a slim loss to the Denver Nuggets on December 18. Though Love's streak of 14 or more rebounds ended in that loss, he would figure himself in double-digit rebounding all the way to March 18, 2011.

On January 3, 2011, Kevin Love had another game of at least 20 rebounds as he collected 24 of them while scoring 12 markers in a loss to the Boston Celtics. He followed that up by scoring at least 30 in two consecutive games. Love had 35 points, 15 rebounds, and five assists on the Charlotte Bobcats. He then had 30 points and 19 boards against the Portland Trailblazers. Two games after that, he had 20 points and 20 rebounds in a loss to the Spurs. On January 26, Kevin had another 30-20 game as he finished a loss to the Oklahoma City Thunder with 31 points and 21 rebounds. In that overtime classic, he battled it out with Kevin Durant, who had 47 in the game. Love shot 13 out of 23 from the floor and had eight offensive rebounds in that match.

During the month of January 2011, Love averaged 23.6 points on 53% shooting and 16 rebounds. His 3-point shooting also developed into a lethal weapon, and Love began to take more of those shots, which made him an even more devastating offensive weapon. He entered February with the same kind of monstrous performances as his streak of double-doubles continued. Despite his excellent performances, Kevin Love was not initially selected as an All-Star for the Western Conference. It was probably because the Timberwolves only won 11 games heading into the All-Star break. However, a spot opened up as Yao Ming could not participate due to injury. David Stern chose Kevin Love to replace the injured Chinese center to play as an All-Star. With that, Kevin Love was an All-Star for the very first time in his career.

After his first All-Star selection, Love would not slow down. Shortly after the midseason break, he had 37 points and 23 rebounds in a win versus the Golden State Warriors. He was 8 out of 13 from the floor, 3 out of 4 from three-point territory, and 18 out of 23 from the foul line in that game. In his second game in March, he had 20 points and 20 boards in an 11-point win versus the Detroit Pistons. Love followed that up by posting 21 points and 23 rebounds in a win against the Philadelphia 76ers. He rounded up a three-game streak of 20-20 games by finishing with 20 points and 21 rebounds in a loss to the Washington Wizards on March 5. Love would post one more 20-rebound game on March 9 when he had 21 boards in a big win against the Indiana Pacers.

While his 30-30 game showed his potential dominance over the course of a single game, Love also set another record which showed his ability over an entire NBA season. In a streak lasting from November to March, Kevin Love grabbed a double-double of points and rebounds for 53 straight games. It was the longest stretch since Elvin Hayes in 1974. His streak ended on March 20 when he suffered a strained groin against the Kings. He would only play two more games after that injury. Had Love stayed healthy, we surely would have seen him breaking Hayes record of 55 straight double-double games.

After the double-double streak ended, Love played just three more games for the rest of the regular seasons before sitting out with nagging injuries. By doing so, he showed that while the Timberwolves had won very few games with him, they were far worse without him. With Love sitting out, Minnesota lost 15 straight games to finish the 2010-11 season. After winning 15 games in 2009-10, they won just 17 in 2010-11. Love finished his first star season averaging 20.2 points, a league-leading 15.2 points, and 2.5 assists. He was the NBA's Most Improved Player. It was evident that his conditioning had improved as he played nearly 36 minutes per game after playing less than 30 in both of his first two seasons in the NBA. His overall offense and his three-point shooting also significantly improved as he shot 47% from the floor and 41.7% from beyond the arc.

Despite his monstrous numbers, Love would miss the postseason for the third straight season.

Breakout Scoring Season

During the offseason, the Wolves made their biggest move in the year by firing Rambis and replacing him with Rick Adelman. Adelman was a highly respected coach who had led Clyde Drexler's Trail Blazers and, later, the famous 2002 Sacramento Kings. He was known as a skilled offensive coach with a personality which worked well with most NBA players. With Adelman replacing Rambis, the long-awaited arrival of prized Spanish point guard Ricky Rubio and number 2 draft pick Derrick Williams, things were beginning to look up for the long-suffering Timberwolves. Love, the new face of the franchise, had a lot of things to be happy about as he was finally reinforced with a lot of help heading into the lockout-shortened 66-game season.

However at the start of the 2011-12 season, David Kahn made a decision that may have cost them Love's respect and future services. After three years in the NBA, Kevin

Love was eligible for an extension from the Timberwolves. Minnesota could offer a 5-year, $80 million contract to one player on their team, and everyone assumed that Kahn would give it to Love after his stellar 2010-11 performance. However, Kahn refused.

He was interested in saving the 5-year deal for Rubio even though he obviously had no way of knowing whether Rubio would be worth that much money four years from that point. It is highly likely that Kahn's decision was because he had drafted Rubio in 2009, while Kevin McHale had drafted Love in 2008. Rather than do what was best for the Timberwolves, Kahn likely wanted to make sure that he got credit for eventually turning Minnesota into a championship team – which meant that Rubio had to be the star of the Timberwolves instead of Love. Thanks to Kahn's decision, Kevin Love instead signed an extension for just four additional years, along with an opt-out clause in the fourth year. Had David Kahn given Love the 5-year deal that he deserved, Kevin Love would almost assuredly still be with the Minnesota Timberwolves today.

On the basketball court, Kevin Love continued to show that he was in fact a true star that season. He started the season with a double-double game against the Thunder on December 26, 2011. He had 22 points and 12 boards in that loss. In the next game, he had 31 points and 20 rebounds in a narrow loss to the Milwaukee Bucks. Love would continue rebounding in double digits up until January 21. He was proving to the world that his great rebounding year during the previous season was not a fluke.

While Love's rebounding prowess was always a constant ever since he entered the NBA, what was surprising in that early part of the season was that his offense had improved considerably. In his 15-game double-double streak to start the 2011-12 season, Love scored at least 20 points in all but two games. He also had three consecutive games of scoring 30 or more points. Love had 34 points as he hit 17 out of 18 free throws in a win versus the New Orleans Hornets. He then had 30 points on 12 out of 26 shooting in a loss to the Atlanta Hawks. Finally, he had 33 points versus the Sacramento Kings in a 13-point win.

In a game against the newly emergent Los Angeles Clippers and their star power forward Blake Griffin on January 20, 2012, Love helped the Wolves rally from a 15-point deficit and hit a 3-point game-winning buzzer beater over Clippers center DeAndre Jordan. On January 23, Love continued to score great as he put up 39 points in a loss to the Houston Rockets. He had 39 points and 11 rebounds in that game. Kevin shot 13 out of 19 from the field, 5 out of 5 from the three-point line, and 8 out of 10 from the foul stripe in that game. He would have 31 points in the next game, shooting 9 out of 16 from the floor and 4 out of 6 from downtown in that 15-point win versus the Dallas Mavericks. After that performance, he had 18 points and 16 rebounds in a win versus the San Antonio Spurs. Love finished that stretch with a 33-point game in a loss to the Los Angeles Lakers.

Love started February 2012 on a good note as he continued to put up more than 20 points per game along with double-digit rebounding. He had 25 points and 18 rebounds in a nine-point win versus the Houston Rockets. Kevin shot 9 out of 16 from the field in that game while grabbing 7 offensive rebounds. However, he would miss two straight games as he was suspended for an altercation involving Luis Scola of the Rockets. In the next two games, Kevin Love had consecutive performances of putting up 32 points. In those games, he combined for 19 out of 39 from the field and a perfect 24 out of 24 from the free throw line. In the second game of that two-game stretch, he had 21 rebounds as he grabbed 18 defensive boards.

Love would not stop there. He would have another pair of consecutive 30-point games. He had 30 points and 18 rebounds in a win against the Charlotte Hornets on February 15. He then had 33 points and 17 boards as they Wolves won by 13 against the Rockets on February 17. He shot a combined total of 22 out of 37 from the field and 15 out of 18 from the foul line in those two big wins. Kevin Love rounded up an 11-game double-double streak on February 22. Kevin Love was a no-brainer for the Western Conference All-Stars that season. He also bested Kevin Durant in the finals of the 2012 Three-Point Shootout to be anointed as that season's three-point champion.

Shortly after the All-Star break, Kevin Love had 42 points and ten rebounds in a win versus the Portland Trailblazers. He made 15 out of 27 shots from the field and 5 out of 8 from beyond the arc in that game. He then had 39 points and 17 rebounds as he defeated Blake Griffin's team once again on March 5. He shot 13 out of 25 from the field and 5 out of 10 from outside the three-point arc in that game. At that point, it seemed like Kevin Love and the Timberwolves were on the right track to make a playoff spot if their fortunes were aligned. He would then have 29 points and 16 rebounds as the Warriors won against Portland by 12 points.

But it was misfortune which struck instead. On March 9, 2012, Ricky Rubio tore his ACL. Rubio had shown to be an excellent passing point guard and made a strong offensive pairing with Kevin Love. Love's tremendous shooting ability compensated for Rubio's inability to score, while Rubio took care of the ball handling and passing which Love could not. Montenegrin center Nikola Pekovic also developed to become a better center than Darko

Milicic. Still with Rubio gone, Love was once again stuck carrying a team that was just not good enough.

Despite the loss of Ricky Rubio, Kevin Love was still playing at a superstar level. He had 31 points and 16 rebounds in a loss to the Hornets after Rubio's injury. He then had 25 points and 16 boards in a narrow loss to the Utah Jazz on March 15. From that point, he started a 10-game run of double-doubles. On March 19, Love posted 36 points and 16 rebounds in a win against the Golden State Warriors. He made 13 out of 23 from the field in that game and shot 3 out of 5 from the three-point arc.

On March 23, in a game against the eventual Western Conference Champion Oklahoma City Thunder, Love scored 51 points and carried the team for two overtimes. He also had 14 rebounds in that classic game. Love made 16 out of 27 shots from the field and 7 out of 11 from beyond the arc in that game. He also made 12 out of 16 free throws. Nevertheless, Oklahoma City still won 149-140, and a frustrated Love brushed off his game by noting that they had lost. Kevin Durant and Russell Westbrook combined for 85 points in that game as Love was almost a one-man team playing against two of the best young superstars in the NBA.

Despite a loss in his career game, Kevin Love immediately bounced back in his next game in a win against the Denver Nuggets. The superstar power forward put up 30 points and 21 rebounds as he shot 11 out of 19 in 44 minutes that night. Three days later, he put up 40 points and 19 rebounds in a five-point win versus the Charlotte Bobcats on March 28. He made 14 out of 31 shots from the floor and 4 out of 7 from the arc.

However, without Rubio, the Wolves fell apart down the stretch. Despite monstrous double-double numbers, Kevin Love would and the Wolves would lose in the superstar forward's final seven games. Love once again sat out the final stretch of games with various injuries and Minnesota won just 4 of their final 22 games. Kevin Love finished the season averaging a then career-best 26 points, 13.3 rebounds, and two assists. He played 39 minutes per game while shooting about 45% from the field.

Love was nominated to the All-NBA Second Team for the first time in his career. Even though Minnesota had faded down the stretch, their 26-40 record was the team's best performance in six seasons. Just like last year, there was room for optimism – though it was marred both by concerns over Rubio's recovery and the fact that thanks to Kahn's bad extension decision, Minnesota would need to assemble a winning team as quickly as possible. They picked up wings like Chase Budinger, Andrei Kirilenko, and Brandon Roy to bolster their team and hoped to make the playoffs.

Injury Season

Unfortunately, Kevin Love's season was tainted by a hand injury. Three weeks before the 2012-13 season began, Love broke his right hand doing knuckle push-ups. Though it was admirable for Love to continue working hard on his conditioning and physique, the injury kept him out for the first nine games of the season. He was supposed to be out for as much as a month. However, Kevin surprised everyone when he made an early return. That's a testament to how much of a competitor Kevin Love is. When Love returned, it was clear that his hand continued to bother him as he hardly got back to playing at the superstar level he's played in the previous two seasons.

Kevin Love made his season debut on November 21, 2012 in a loss to the Denver Nuggets. Love put up 34 points and grabbed 14 rebounds as he never showed signs of slowing down, especially since he shot 48% from the field in that game. He then had 24 points and 13 rebounds in the next game as the Wolves lost by eight points to the Portland Trailblazers.

Love's rebounding continued to be as dominant as ever. He grabbed 24 points in a game against the Sacramento Kings on November 27. He had 21 defensive boards in that game as the Wolves' defense seemed on point in that eight-point win. Love also had 23 points in that outing. Kevin Love would start his season rebounding in double digits in his first 10 games. In one of those games, he had 36 points and 13 rebounds in an 18-point win against the Cleveland Cavaliers on December 7.

On December 20, Love put up 28 points, 11 rebounds, and seven assists in a win against the Oklahoma City Thunder. That was just after grabbing 18 rebounds versus the powerhouse Miami Heat team. However, it seemed like Kevin Love's injury was getting to him as he missed two games in December. Even when he was playing, it looked like he couldn't perform at his best. In a three-point loss to Houston, Love shot 3 out of 14 from the field for only 7 points. He did have 12 rebounds.

After that dreadful game on December 26, Love bounced back three days later to score 23 points and grab 18 rebounds in a win versus the Phoenix Suns. However, the hand would bother him once again as Kevin would combine for merely 8 out of 27 from the field in the next two games. The only thing that wasn't bothered was his rebounding abilities as he combined for 27 rebounds in those two bad games. Kevin Love would reinjure his hand in the second game of that terrible shooting stretch. The fracture required Love to undergo surgery.

Kevin was the topic of criticisms because of that injury because many people thought he had returned too quickly after injuring his hand for the first time before the season. Although the injury and the recovery period had slated him to come back after as much as 10 weeks, Love never returned to the Wolves' lineup that season. He averaged 18.3 points, 14 rebounds, and 2.3 assists that season. However, the hand injury had apparently bothered Love's scoring as he averaged 35.2% from the field and 21.7% from beyond the arc.

Love was not the only Minnesota player to suffer from injury. Rubio missed over a month of the regular season as he recovered from his ACL tear and was not as good as his rookie year even when he did return. Chase Budinger played for only 23 games; Brandon Roy played just five, and Nikola Pekovic missed 20. The only Minnesota player who started more than 65 games in the 2012-13 season was guard Luke Ridnour. The constant injuries meant that players were always being switched in and out of the lineup, which prevented good team chemistry from forming. Despite the games missed with injury, the Timberwolves still managed to win 31 games that year, which was almost as good as their record last season. Had

Love, Kirilenko, and Rubio been healthy for the entire 2012-13 season, it is possible that the Timberwolves could have reached the playoffs.

Unfortunately after five years in the NBA, Love's frustration with the Timberwolves was now a legitimate problem. Renowned Yahoo Sports journalist Adrian Wojnarowski wrote in a December 2012 column that Love was, among other things, frustrated by David Kahn's lack of a plan and upset how Minnesota management had initially disbelieved his story of getting injured by doing push-ups. Love did not want just to be part of a squad which made the playoffs. He wanted to be on a contending team, whether it was with the Timberwolves or another team.

Back to Superstar Form, Final Season in Minnesota

In May 2013, the Timberwolves finally fired David Kahn. Flip Saunders, who had coached the last Minnesota team to make the playoffs in 2004, took over as the new general manager. Saunders picked up scoring guard Kevin Martin and swingman Corey Brewer for defensive purposes. Minnesota's roster of Rubio, Love, Martin, and Pekovic made it clear what their strategy was. The Timberwolves sought to outscore rather than out-defend their opponents, especially behind Rick Adelman's offensive talents. While it was unclear whether Minnesota could finally return to the 2013 NBA Playoffs, it was widely expected that they would remain competitive for that eighth and final slot. A great deal rested now on the shoulder of Kevin Love.

Love would start the season with 31 points and 17 rebounds in a five-point win versus the Orlando Magic. He made 8 out of 19 from the floor and 12 out of 16 from the foul line in that game. The Wolves would then beat the Thunder by 19 points in their second game on November 1, 2013. Love had 24 points and 12 rebounds in that match. The Timberwolves then finished a 3-0 start to their season as Love put up 34 points, 15 rebounds, and five assists versus the New York Knicks. Love made 10 of 19 shots from the field and 12 out of 15 from the foul stripe.

The Wolves would lose two straight games after that good start. However, the losses were not because of a lack of effort on the part of Minnesota's superstar power forward. Love combined for 42 points, 29 rebounds, and 11 assists in those two games. After those losses, the Timberwolves went back to work. Love had 32 points, 15 rebounds, and eight assists in an eight-point win versus the Dallas Mavericks. He shot 12 out of 21 from the field while matching up with Dirk Nowitzki. Love then had 25 points and 13 rebounds in a 25-point drubbing of the Los Angeles Lakers on November 10. Love then had 23 points and 19 rebounds in a loss to the Clippers. They went back to the winning track by winning against the Cavaliers by 29 points. Love had 33 points, eight rebounds, and eight assists in that game.

At that point, it seemed like the Wolves were on their way to a playoff spot. But from there, things began to fall steadily apart. Every Minnesota player outside of Love possessed a glaring weakness, whether it was Kevin Martin's inability to defend, Corey Brewer's inability to shoot, or Ricky Rubio's inability to score. Outside of Rubio, they were a poor fit alongside Love. In addition to the problems which surrounded the players, Rick Adelman was distracted for much of the season by his wife's ill health and repeatedly missed games to watch over her.

Despite those setbacks, Kevin Love tried his best to shoulder the burden on his broad shoulders. He continued putting up double-double games like it was an early morning coffee for him. In his first 20 games, Love had 19 double-double outings. He had four games of scoring at least 30 games in those 20 outings. He even rebounded 15 or more rebounds in nine outings of his 19 double-double games in that stretch.

On December 13, Love put up a then-season high of 42 points in a loss to the San Antonio Spurs. He also grabbed 14 boards in that game. Kevin made 15 out of 27 from the floor and 8 out of 9 from the three-point line in that match. In the game after that, he put up 30 points and grabbed nine rebounds versus the Memphis Grizzlies in an eight-point win. He then flirted with a triple-double on December 18 in a win against the Portland Trailblazers. Love had 29 points, 15 rebounds, and nine assists in that win. Matched up against Blake Griffin and the LA Clippers on December 22, Kevin had 45 points, 19 rebounds, and six assists in a narrow loss to the Clips. He made 15 of 23 shots from the field and 13 out of 15 from the foul stripe in that game.

After that loss to the Clippers, Love and the Wolves got back to the winning column as they won two consecutive games. The superstar forward had 25 points and 11 rebounds versus the Washington Wizards in a 22-point win. They then won by the same amount in the next game versus the Milwaukee Bucks. Kevin Love went for 33 points, 13 rebounds, and six assists in that game. Though it came at a loss, Love had 36 points and 11 rebounds versus the Dallas Mavericks in their next game on December 30.

Entering 2014, Kevin Love continued to play well. On January 4, 2014, he had 30 points, 14 rebounds, and five assists versus the Oklahoma City Thunder. There seems to be something in the Thunder that allows Love to always play well against them. From that point on until the end of January, Love would have 11 double-double games out of the 16 games he played that month. In two of those games, he almost had his first career double-double. Kevin had 19 points, 13 rebounds, and seven assists on January 21 in a win versus Utah. He then had 26 points, 14 boards, and eight dimes versus Golden State on January 24.

On February 1, Love went for 43 points and 19 rebounds versus the Atlanta Hawks. In that loss, he made 12 out of 22 shots from the field and 17 out of 18 from the foul line. In the next game just three days after, Kevin had 31 points and 17 rebounds as the Wolves took a game against the LA Lakers. As the All-Star break was nearing, Love had consecutive double-double games while scoring 30 or more points. He had 31 points and ten rebounds against the Rockets on February 10 before putting up 32 points, 11 rebounds, and eight assists in the win versus the Denver Nuggets on February 12. As the midseason classic dawned, Love saw a return to the All-Star game. It was his third selection.

Love would get back to work after the midseason break. He had 42 points and 16 rebounds as he shot 14 out of 22 from the field and 5 out of 10 from beyond the arc in a big win versus the Indiana Pacers on February 19. He then had his first triple-double game against the Utah Jazz in a win on February 22. Kevin Love put up 37 points, 12 rebounds, and ten dimes in that game wherein he shot 11 out of 20 from the field and 6 out of 10 from outside the three-point line. He would then have 31 points and ten rebounds in a loss to the Blazers. On February 25, he almost had another triple-double as Love put up 33 points, 13 rebounds, and nine assists in a win in Phoenix before putting up 22 points, ten rebounds, and seven assists in Sacramento. On March 3, Love and the Wolves finished that road trip in Denver, where Kevin put up 33 points and 19 assists. The Wolves were 5-1 in that six-game stretch.

On March 9, Kevin Love flirted with another triple-double as he finished a loss to the Toronto Raptors with 26 points, 11 rebounds, and nine assists. He then had 35 points in a one-point win in Dallas on March 19 before putting up another near triple-double game on March 23 against the Suns. Love had 36 points, 14 rebounds, and nine assists in that match. Kevin completed his second career triple-double on March 28 in a blowout win versus the Lakers. He had 22 points, ten rebounds, and ten assists. On April 2, Kevin had 24 points, 16 rebounds, and ten assists for his third triple-double against the Memphis Grizzlies.

Kevin Love would explode for 43 points and 11 rebounds on April 13 in a narrow loss to the Sacramento Kings. He hit 12 out of 23 from the field and shot 15 out of 17 from the free-throw line in that game. In the next game, Love had another great output as he went for 40 points, 14 rebounds, and nine assists on the Golden State Warriors in a loss. Love finished the regular season by flirting with another triple-double of 19 points, ten rebounds, and nine assists.

However, for much of the 2013-14 season, the Timberwolves were what sportswriter Zach Harper called, "ineffectively good." When they won games, they won them by large margins. In close games, the Timberwolves repeatedly faded down the stretch and choked in the clutch.

Why did Minnesota lose so many close games? Some pointed out that Minnesota's primary wing scorer, Kevin Martin, had a long history of not showing up in the clutch. Some argued that the Timberwolves just suffered from awful luck. Others said that Adelman's growing disinterest in coaching hurt the team down the stretch, but a lot of people blamed Kevin Love.

Initially, the idea of blaming Love for Minnesota's inability to win seems absurd. Love had returned to his old form in 2011-12 when he had made the All-NBA Second Team. Love was once again a member of the All-NBA Second Team as he averaged 26.1 points, 12.5 rebounds, and a career-high 4.4 assists over the NBA season and had plenty of big performances. You also couldn't blame him as an efficient scorer because he was finished fourth in scoring that season with shooting clips of 45.7% from the floor and 37.6% from beyond the arc. Given everything Love had accomplished, how could he be blamed for Minnesota's inability to win?

The response was to analyze Love's skill set. It was true that Love had many points and rebounds. However, he had begun relying on his 3-point shot more compared to previous season. He took 6.6 3-pointers per game, the highest of his career by a significant margin. If Love's game relied on 3-pointers and tipping the ball in on offensive rebounds to score, then how could he score by himself when Minnesota needed him the most? Regardless of whether such claims were true or not, Minnesota continued to struggle in close games throughout the entire season. At the end of the season, they finished with a 40-42 record. While it was Minnesota's best season since 2004-05, they were nowhere near making the playoffs in the competitive Western Conference. The gamble had failed. As Love could become a free agent in 2015, it was almost all but assured that Minnesota would trade Love now during the 2014 offseason. But where would he go? NBA teams like Golden State and the Lakers lined up to entice Love to their team. When Love visited Boston during the offseason, sports fans assumed that it meant that he would join the Boston Celtics.

Joining the Cleveland Cavaliers, Forming the Big Three with LeBron and Kyrie

In the offseason before the 2014-15 season, LeBron James decided to leave the Miami Heat and rejoin the Cleveland Cavaliers. Everything changed with that simple decision. Cleveland had won three number 1 picks over the past four years and had drafted the highly anticipated Andrew Wiggins in the 2014 NBA Draft. A trio of James, Wiggins, and Irving would have been a good one. However, Wiggins was a still a raw rookie. LeBron wanted to win a title for Cleveland immediately. He didn't have time to wait for a rookie to develop. They had to make moves for Kevin Love, who was intent on leaving Minnesota. On August 23, 2014, the Minnesota Timberwolves traded Love to the Cavaliers in exchange for Wiggins and 2013 #1 draft pick Anthony Bennett. With LeBron, Love, and point guard Kyrie Irving, the Cavaliers have become a powerhouse team in the Eastern Conference.

Since Kevin Love's third season in the NBA, he never had to play second fiddle to anyone. Even in the second half of his sophomore season, he was already a designated guy in the Timberwolves' roster. He was always the one scoring and rebounding the ball. Love would bully players down at the low post or even take them out to shoot three shots outside the arc. In a lot of situations, he was even playing the role of a playmaker as he knew how to utilize his excellent passing abilities. But how could he blend in Cleveland?

Love joined a Cleveland Cavaliers' team that had three ball-heavy players. LeBron James almost always needed the ball in his hands to be effective. He could score against any defense or would make plays for other teammates with his unique quarterbacking skills. Kyrie Irving was a scoring point guard that needed the ball to break defenses down with what is widely regarded as the best ball handler in the whole NBA. Off the bench, even Dion Waiters needed a lot of touches to become effective. Even when he couldn't score, Love was always a supreme rebounder. But he was joining a team that also had great rebounders such as Anderson Varejao and Tristan Thompson. Under new head Coach David Blatt's system in the Cavs, it seemed like Kevin Love was a lost piece.

Despite playing third fiddle to the likes of LeBron and Kyrie, Love was still capable of putting up great numbers on the board. In his first game as a Cavalier, Kevin Love put up 19 points, 14 rebounds, and four assists in 38 minutes. However, Cleveland lost that game to the Knicks. He then had 16 points and 16 boards as the Cavs won their second game. Love posted 22 markers and ten boards as the Cavaliers were blown out of Portland. Despite playing well behind 'Bron and Kyrie, Love was still adjusting to the new system and his new teammates.

Kevin Love would score in double digits in his first ten games that season. Six of those games were double-doubles. His season high at that point was 22 points in a tight win versus the New Orleans Pelicans. Love made six three-pointers in that match. However, Cleveland could only win half of those ten games. It was clear that whatever they were doing wasn't working. On November 22, 2014, Kevin had a new season high as a Cavs player when he put up 23 points in a loss to Toronto. Just a week later, he had 28 points and ten rebounds against the Indiana Pacers. The game after that, he had 27 points and 11 rebounds as he hit four three-pointers out of eight attempts. Kevin Love finished a five-game double-double streak in a win against the Brooklyn Nets. He had 19 points and 14 boards in that game. The Cavs were in the middle of an eight-game streak at that point.

On December 15, Kevin Love would go for 22 points, 19 rebounds, five assists, and four steals in a win against the Charlotte Hornets. However, Love would find himself in the background of things a few games later as the Cavs would still win games without him contributing a lot of points or even a lot of rebounds. Even when Love was putting up monstrous numbers, the Cavaliers would somehow struggle to win. Exhibit A to that is when Cleveland lost six straight games in early January.

On January 4, 2015 of that six-game skid, Love had 30 points and ten boards versus the Mavericks. He then had 28 points and 19 rebounds in Philadelphia before putting up 17 markers and 16 rebounds versus the Houston Rockets. Love then had 25 points and ten boards against the Warriors on January 11 before ending the skid with 9 points and nine rebounds. After breaking the losing streak on January 15, Kevin Love would sit out one game, which the Cavaliers won.

Since coming back from a one-game absence, Kevin Love became a part of a 12-game Cleveland Cavaliers winning streak. However, it was a different Kevin Love as he found himself shooting more three-pointers than he ever did before. His minutes also dropped as David Blatt would prefer playing the defensive-minded Tristan Thompson instead of him, or would even put LeBron at the power forward spot for more speed. Despite that, Kevin Love was still putting up good stats from here and there.

In a win against the Utah Jazz on January 21, Kevin Love had 19 points and 13 rebounds. He made only one three-pointer out of seven attempts in that game. Four days later, he had the same numbers but made 5 out of 7 three-pointers instead in a win against the OKC Thunder. Against Sacramento, he had 23 points and ten rebounds. In their 12th straight victory on February 5, Love put up 24 points and nine rebounds against the Clippers. Three days later, Love had a new season high of 32 points together with 10 boards against the struggling Los Angeles Lakers. He made 11 out of 18 from the field and 7 out of 8 three-pointers in that game. Despite playing well as a third option, Kevin Love was not an All-Star that season.

On February 24, Kevin scored 24 points and grabbed nine rebounds in a win against the Detroit Pistons. He tied a career high of 8 made three-pointers that game. After that game, Love found himself seeing fewer touches and fewer minutes up to the end of the season. He merely scored at least 20 points five more times since then. His rebounding numbers weren't eye-popping either as he figured in double-digit rebounding only nine out of the next 20 games that he played. His next great game came on March 10 in a win over the Dallas Mavericks. Kevin Love had 24 points and 14 rebounds in that 33-point win.

At the end of the 2014-15 season, Kevin Love averaged 16.4 points, 9.7 rebounds, and 2.2 assists. His scoring saw a near 10-point dip from the previous season. Love shot 43.4% from the floor and 36.7% from the three-point line. As you can see, Love's numbers were down from his previous four seasons. One reason that happened was that he was playing third fiddle to the likes of LeBron James and Kyrie Irving. When the Cavs acquired JR Smith in a midseason trade, Love's touches didn't improve as he was playing alongside three ball-dominant players. Also, one problem Kevin Love had in playing alongside LeBron and Kyrie was the fact that he was underutilized. David Blatt was using him as a stretch power forward that camped all day outside the perimeter. The purpose of which was to give James and Irving wide open spaces to drive to the basket. However, that hurt Love's scoring as the only times he could put up points was when the two playmakers dish the ball out to him for perimeter shots. Love could have been used more effectively as his low post scoring was one of the best for a power forward in the whole NBA.

It's a given that Love's scoring numbers would dip as he was playing alongside two great scorers. What was surprising was that his rebounding also decreased. That's also another given outcome since he was playing with the likes of Tristan Thompson, Anderson Varejao, and, later, Timofey Mozgov, who are all good rebounders. However, one other aspect you have to look at was the fact that Kevin Love was always camping out on the perimeter to stretch the defense. That hindered him from getting great position inside the paint for offensive rebounds, an aspect of his game that seemed second to none. He was limited to merely 1.9 offensive boards that season. Love's assist numbers also dipped because the ball was always in the hands of his two other superstar teammates.

Though Kevin Love was underachieving and was underutilized in the Cleveland Cavaliers, the team won 53 games that season and were the second seed in the Eastern Conference heading into the postseason. Kevin Love was not posting up superstar numbers, but what was more important was that he was on his way to the playoffs for the very first time in seven professional years in the NBA. In those seven years, he's seen three All-Star appearances and two All-NBA Second Team selections. He's even won the Most Improved Player award. But he's never seen a playoff minute as a member of the Timberwolves. With the Cavs, he finally saw a postseason appearance. Moreover, he had a legitimate chance of winning an NBA championship.

Kevin Love and the Cleveland Cavaliers were a favorite to make it all the way to the Eastern Conference Finals. However, it didn't mean that their path to the third round wouldn't be as smooth as they would think. In the opening round, the Cavs faced the young Boston Celtics, a team without any superstar, but had a lot of excellent players. Cleveland drew first blood in Game 1 as Kevin Love posted 19 points and 12 rebounds. Though it was merely

Love's first ever playoff game, he already played well with a double-double as he got the win.

In Game 2, Love was limited to playing his usual role for the Cavs as a stretch power forward. He attempted five shots from beyond the three-point line, but only converted one of them. Moreover, as he was playing on the perimeter for the majority of his 29 minutes of action, he only had six rebounds in that game. Luckily, Love wasn't the only superstar in Cleveland as the Cavs took Game 2 by 8 points. The result in Game 3 was similar. However, Kevin Love posted a playoff career high in that game. Love converted six of his ten three-point shot attempts to score 23 points on a total of 8 out of 16 from the floor. He also had nine rebounds in that game as his team were up 3-0 in the series.

After winning Game 3, Kevin Love and the Cavs were assured to move past to the second round since no team in NBA history has ever come back from a 0-3 deficit to win a seven-game series. Love, in only his first appearance in the playoffs, was on his way to the second round in a relatively straightforward manner. However fate, with a little help from a long-haired 7-footer in Boston, turned things for the worst for Kevin Love.

In Game 4, with just about 6 minutes left in the first quarter, Kevin Love was matched up with the Celtics' 7-footer Kelly Olynyk. In a rebound situation, the two big men got tangled up with one another. Olynyk, in an attempt to stop the superior rebounder from getting to the ball, grabbed Love's left arm and pulled him away. Kevin Love winced in pain after that incident as he rushed over to the locker room. He would not return to the very physical game that saw tempers rising from guys like Kendrick Perkins and JR Smith. In the end, the Cavaliers won the game and were headed to the second round via a four-game sweep versus the Celtics.

After the win against the Celtics, Kevin Love was assessed to have suffered a dislocated left shoulder. He would call out Olynyk's act as a dirty play that was committed on purpose. While we may not know whether the act was actually pre-meditated, Love's words might have just been born out from the frustrations of facing an injury when the Cavs needed him most and when he was on his way to the second round in his first playoff appearance. It was indeed a tragic incident on the part of Kevin, who was simply happy about making the playoffs for the very first time since joining the NBA in 2008.

Kevin's dislocated shoulder would keep him out of the entirety of the postseason as the Cavs defeated the Bulls and the Hawks to make it to the NBA Finals. The team made it all the way to the championship round without much challenged as Tristan Thompson stepped up in Love's place to play terrific defense and to provide the same type of energy in rebounding. Cleveland would lose to the Golden State Warriors in six games in the Finals. Had Love been there together with Kyrie Irving, who was injured in Game 1 of that series, things might have been different as LeBron James was left with the task of carrying the whole team on his back.

On Top of the Eastern Conference

Before the start of the 2015-16 season, the Cleveland Cavaliers had learned that they had to play handicapped for much of the beginning of the new season. Star point guard Kyrie Irving was still recovering from the injury he suffered in Game 1 of the 2015 NBA Finals while role player Iman Shumpert was also out with an injury. The good thing was that the Cavs acquired veteran point guard Mo Williams to start in place of the injured superstar playmaker. They also signed veteran wingman Richard Jefferson to back LeBron up at the small forward spot and to provide a lot of experience to the squad. Despite the acquisitions of two veteran scorers, Kyrie's injury meant that Love would have to shoulder more offensive load than he did in his first season with the Cavs.

In an opening day loss the Chicago Bulls, Kevin Love put up 18 points, eight rebounds, and four assists in a game that ended with Pau Gasol blocking a possible game-tying shot by LeBron. Love hit 3 out of 7 three-pointers in that match. In the second game of the season, Love posted 17 points and 13 rebounds for his first double-double of the season. He shot 50% from the field in that game as Cleveland won in Memphis by 30 big points. Love would record a then-season high of 24 points, 14 rebounds, and five assists in a win against the Miami Heat on October 30,

2015. He hit 3 of 7 attempts from beyond the arc in that game.

Though Kevin Love's scoring was a bit sporadic to start the season, he did come back to that rebounding monster form he was in when he played in Minnesota. The reason for that was that Tristan Thompson, a great rebounder and defender at the power forward position, could not join the team in training camp because of contract extension disputes. He found it difficult to gel with the Cavs at the start of the season because he missed the entire training camp. Love was left to play the rebounding role more than what David Blatt had him do in his first season with the team.

From November 4 until 8, Kevin Love had a three-game streak of double-doubles. He had 11 points and 12 rebounds against the Knicks before putting up 12 points and 14 boards versus the struggling Philadelphia 76ers. He finished that stretch by scoring 22 points and collecting 19 rebounds in a win against the Indiana Pacers. He scored 22 in the next game before being limited to 7 in New York on November 13. The Cleveland Cavaliers completed an eight-game winning streak after dropping the opening game to Chicago. In a loss that ended the streak, Love had 24 points and 14 rebounds in Milwaukee. He hit 4 out of 9 three-pointers in that game and was 8 out of 18 from the field overall.

After that loss to Milwaukee, Kevin Love scored in double digits in the next seven games. He had at least 20 points in six of those games. Love had 22 points and 15 rebounds as they took revenge against the Bucks on November 19. He then scored 25 points and grabbed 11 rebounds versus Atlanta before going for 34 big points in a win against the Orlando Magic. Love made 6 out of 9 three-pointers in that game. He would make five three-pointers in a loss to Toronto as he went for 21 points and 13 rebounds. Love finished that eight-game streak of double-doubles by putting up 18 points and 16 rebounds in a win versus the Charlotte Hornets on November 27.

December didn't start well for Love and the Cleveland Cavaliers as they found themselves losing the first three games of that month. In those three losses, Love combined for merely 28 points on 10 out of 36 shooting from the field. His rebounding wasn't excellent either as he figured in double digits in that department only once in those three setbacks.

After that, Love went back to scoring well as the Cavs won six straight games. Love was in double digits in all but one of those wins. On December 12, in a win against the Boston Celtics, he had 20 points as he shot 7 out of 16 from the field and 3 out of 7 from the three-point line. In the end game of that streak, Kevin Love had 23 points and 13 rebounds in a win versus the New York Knicks. Love made 8 out of 17 shots in that game. In the next game on Christmas Day, the Cavaliers faced the Golden State Warriors in a much-anticipated rematch of the 2015 NBA Finals. Love was aching to play in that game as he missed the championship series. However, he struggled against the Warriors' defense as he shot 5 out of 16 for 10 points. He did, however, grab 18 big rebounds in that loss.

When Kyrie Irving returned in December, Kevin Love's touches and his scoring suddenly dropped as he was relegated to playing the third fiddle and floor stretcher with James and Irving on the floor. However, he still did whatever was asked of him to do. In the middle of January 2016, Love had four straight double-double games. Though he did not score well in any of those games, he still contributed with his rebounding. He had 15 points, 15 rebounds, and six assists in a win against the 76ers on January 10. Two days later, he put up 15 puts and 12 rebounds in a win against the Dallas Mavericks. After that, he went for 10 points and 12 rebounds in a loss to the San Antonio Spurs. Finally, Love had 11 points and 13 boards in a win against the Houston Rockets to finish 2-1 in the Cavs' Texas trip.

On January 20, Kevin Love put up 17 points and 18 rebounds in a blowout win against the Brooklyn Nets. He was 50% from the floor in that game as he merely attempted three three-pointers. In the next game, Love went for 18 points and 16 rebounds in a 13-point win against the Los Angeles Clippers. In that game, Kevin was 3 of 6 from beyond the arc. That was the second game of a 10-game streak of scoring in double digits.

Love had some good games in that double-digit scoring stretch. He had 21 points and 11 rebounds in a win against the Phoenix Suns on January 27. In the game after that one, he had 29 points as the Cavs won by 8 in Detroit. When the Cavaliers met the second best team in the West, the San Antonio Spurs, Kevin Love put up 21 points and 11 rebounds in a 14-point statement win. He finished a five-game Cleveland Cavalier winning streak by putting up 19 points and eight rebounds in a win in Indiana. In the next four games, the Kevin Love would not play more than 30 minutes per game as new head coach Tyronn Lue was still experimenting with lineup changes. As the All-Star break came, Love missed his second consecutive midseason classic.

In his first game of playing 30 or more minutes in the last five outings, Kevin Love led the Cavaliers to a 29-point win against the Oklahoma City Thunder, one of the teams he's always played well against as history would show. He had 29 points and 11 rebounds in that game. Though he missed all four of his three-point attempts, Love was still efficient from the floor in that game as he made 9 out of 18 shots from the field. Though it came at a loss, Love scored 24 points against the Detroit Pistons on February 22. He made 8 out of 15 shots in that game while converting 3 out of 7 from beyond the arc.

Love would find himself in on and off situations from game to game as the Cavaliers would make situational changes depending on their opponents. There were times when Love was heavily used because of his shooting and scoring abilities. However, there were also days when his minutes dropped in favor of the defensive-minded energy player Tristan Thompson. However, Kevin Love was still a good contributor for the Cavs team that focused heavily on LeBron James' talents.

On March 7 and 9, Love had a pair of double-doubles. He scored 14 points and grabbed 11 rebounds in a loss to Memphis before putting up 17 markers and ten boards in a win in Sacramento. Kevin would continue to score in double digits until March 18 when the Cavaliers won in Orlando. On March 16, Kevin Love had 23 points and 18 rebounds in a tight win over the Dallas Mavericks. That was after he had consecutive 12-point and 9-rebound games in Los Angeles and then in Utah. On March 23, Love would score 24 points together with ten rebounds and four assists in a win against the Milwaukee Bucks. On March 26, he then had 28 points and 12 rebounds as the Cavs won a battle against the New York Knicks.

As the 2015-16 season goes by, Kevin Love is averaging 15.8 points, 9.9 rebounds, and 2.4 assists. For the second straight season, his shooting numbers seemed too low for a player of his caliber as he mustered only 41.6% from the floor and 34.5% from the three-point line. Despite Love's pedestrian outputs, the Cleveland Cavaliers currently stand on top of the Eastern Conference even after several lineup changes due to injuries and even after a midseason coaching change that saw David Blatt dismissed in favor of Lue. However, none of the Cavalier coaches have been able to utilize Kevin Love to full effect in his two seasons in Cleveland.

Chapter 5: Love's Personal Life

In Love's words, "basketball is my life." He grew up wanting to be an NBA player from the minute he was born and worked his way to becoming one of the best players at the high school, college, and then at the professional level. But even a player as dedicated as Love has found time to enjoy many of the other pleasures in life. In 2011, Love visited China in a 5-day barnstorming trip as part of his new endorsement deal with the Chinese shoe company 361. Love stopped in Beijing, Nanjing, Changsha, Guangzhou, and Shenzhen. He took photos with children, shot baskets, and was amazed by the support that basketball continues to have in China. When Love returned to the United States, he said that if a group of famous American players were to take a tour in China, it might be comparable to when the Beatles visited the United States. No trip has occurred yet, but who knows what Love and his two new superstar teammates may have in mind in the future?

361 is not the only company who has endorsed Love. In 2012, Love participated in Pepsi's "Uncle Drew" commercial alongside his future star teammate Kyrie

Irving. Love put on makeup to look like an old man and took on his middle name, "Wes," to play alongside an old Kyrie Irving and wow a Chicago basketball park. As Kyrie shouted, the two stars, "still got it."

Outside of endorsements and the glitzy world of the NBA, Love has done his best to keep himself grounded. He enjoys hip-hop, a disappointment to his Beach Boys uncle, and has worked in multiple charity projects to assist the needy. Every year with the Timberwolves, Love would collaborate with the Salvation Army to donate coats to the poor – an essential product in the Minnesota winter. Love created a series of short, peculiar videos which advertised the importance of donating coats. These videos, one which had Love declare, "Give me your coats," were regularly played at the Target Center during games, and increased coat donations to the Salvation Army.

Chapter 6: Impact on Basketball

When we look at Kevin Love's impact on a basketball team, there are two questions which should be asked. The simple question is: how does he work? Love seems to be a bit of a contradiction. He is one of the best rebounding power forward in the league, but he is also among the best 3-point shooting big men. How is that possible? And given that Love is not a particularly athletic player, how has he been able to become such a dominant rebounder?

The second question is more analytical. While it is true that Kevin Love's basketball numbers are impressive, the fact is that the Timberwolves have never once come even close to reaching the NBA Playoffs when he was playing in Minnesota. Perhaps bad luck might excuse one or two seasons where the Wolves failed. Given how much a superstar can affect a team in basketball, how can Minnesota's total inability to make the playoffs be explained? Is Kevin Love truly a star?

To answer the first question, we should take a look at another all-time great rebounder and offensive player – Sir

Charles Barkley. While Barkley was faster and much more athletic than Kevin Love, to be one of the great rebounders in NBA history at his true height of 6'4" remains impressive. Barkley took many 3-point shots like Love but was never a good shooter. However, the threat of Barkley's 3-point shot meant that defenders guarded him closely. This allowed Barkley opportunities to drive to the rim and get to the paint to grab his beloved rebounds. Barkley was also a guy who knew how to position himself despite his athletic weaknesses and his lack of size.

Love is similar to Barkley. While he lacks Barkley's athleticism, he has an incredibly strong sense of where to be to grab rebounds. When NBA TV asked him in an interview how he became such a good rebounder, Love said that he uses "his positioning and body" to be relentless on the glass. He also worked to improve his strength upon entering the NBA so that he would not be muscled by more athletic NBA players. Like Barkley, Love knew how to use his body and his natural nose for the ball to get the rebounds despite dwelling outside the perimeter for much of the offensive possession. Those are traits you can never teach players as it would take natural instincts and a high basketball IQ to be at both players' level in rebounding. This answers the question of how Love is a great rebounder and an NBA player. As for the second question about how he has been unable to lead the Timberwolves to the playoffs, we should first remember that Love only had three seasons where he had the opportunity to lead Minnesota in the playoffs. In his first two years in the league, he was developing into a star and was held back by coaching certain factors. In those first two years, Al Jefferson was the main man of the team as he was more polished and more experience as a low post player. In those days, Kevin Love had stamina and conditioning problems that prevented him from playing long minutes on the floor. When he became the leading man on the Wolves' roster, the team was full of young, inexperienced players that could not help alleviate the burden off of Kevin's shoulders. Then in 2012-13, he was unable to play for most of the seasons thanks to his hand injury. Many NBA legends such as Kevin Garnett and Steve Nash have missed the playoffs three times or more in their career. It's not so shameful for Love to miss the postseason in those years.

Moreover, the front office could also be blamed for making questionable decisions. In 2009, they passed on All-Star Stephen Curry to draft Jonny Flynn, who lasted just three years in the NBA. Though Flynn had a respectable rookie season, he is far from the player that Curry is right now. In 2010, they selected Wesley Johnson, who today hangs into the NBA by a mere thread, over star center DeMarcus Cousins. In 2011, they selected Derrick Williams over players like Jonas Valanciunas and Kemba Walker and then sold the pick that became small forward Chandler Parsons to the Houston Rockets. Kevin Love's best teammates during his Minnesota years have been Ricky Rubio and Nikola Pekovic. They are both decent players, but not the sort who become main options on a championship team.

However, that is not to say that Love should not be entirely excused. For all of Love's incredible ability, there are two major concerns about his game which he will need to address now that he is on a Cleveland team that expects nothing less than a championship. The biggest concern is Love's defense. Love has frequently been accused of being so obsessed with rebounds that he slacks on defense in favor to gain an opportunity to grab another rebound. It should be noted that Dennis Rodman, another all-time rebounding legend, also faced this same accusation. However, unlike Rodman, Love isn't even a great post and perimeter defender. He doesn't exert the type of energy that Rodman does on the defensive end of the floor.

Also, Love's lack of athleticism and quickness means that power forwards with range can drive past him to score points close to the basket. The fact that Love played with Pekovic, who is a great scoring center but lacks the size to be a true rim protector, meant that Minnesota throughout Love's tenure was one of the worst teams in stopping points in the paint. Despite Love's height and his length, he is also a bad shot blocker. Throughout his career, he has averaged only 0.5 blocks per game. Love's lack of defense has even led the Cleveland Cavaliers' coaches to favor big defensive guys like Timofey Mozgov and Tristan Thompson to play more minutes though they aren't even half the offensive threat that Love is.

The other concern has been Love's leadership. Leadership is one of the most difficult aspects to measure in sports, and it is far too easy to fall into the trap of assuming that a star player on a bad team must be a bad leader. However, certain incidents in Love's Minnesota years put his leadership ability under scrutiny. In 2012, Love had to be separated from teammate J.J. Barea when they were on the bench in the middle of an NBA game. In January 2014, Love criticized Barea and Dante Cunningham for being seemingly disinterested in the game during the 4th quarter. In May 2014, Ricky Rubio said in a Spanish interview that Love was, "not a leader in voice." Love will not need to lead Cleveland with LeBron James running the show, but there will still be moments when his ability to help guide the rest of the Cavaliers will be crucial.

Despite some of the valid criticisms of Kevin Love, the fact is that he is an excellent player with incredible rebounding ability and a solid scorer. He is also a master of the outlet pass and has repeatedly been compared with his namesake Wes Unseld for his ability to accurately throw the ball down the court to a guard for an easy layup.

Unfortunately, years of incompetent teammates, coaching, and front office management have held Love from being acknowledged as the true superstar that he is. Now that he is on a team with excellent players, there is no doubt that his reputation will improve as the Cavaliers start to win.

Though Love's status did indeed change when he started winning plenty of games with the Cleveland Cavaliers, another criticism began to sprout out. Many began to believe that Love wasn't even a real superstar to begin with. His numbers in Minnesota might have just been a product of the Timberwolves' lack of a go-to-guy on both offense and the rebounding end. There are several reasons for those criticisms.

First, Love was relegated to playing third fiddle to the likes of LeBron James and Kyrie Irving. It is understandable for him to play behind a four-time MVP like LeBron, who is widely considered as the best the world has today. However, one may question why coaches decided to put more emphasis on Kyrie Irving than on Love. Irving's handles are arguably the best in the NBA right now. He's also a great penetrator and an explosive scorer. However, he's more inexperienced than Love is and has achieved less than Kevin has in his career. Because of that, Kevin Love's numbers in Cleveland have significantly dropped as he was given the role of floor spacer.

Second, Love, as a defensive liability, became evident in Cleveland. In his first season with the Cavs, Love was paired with defensive center Anderson Varejao on the frontcourt. After Varejao suffered a season-ending injury, the Cavs' defense suffered primarily because Kevin was sometimes relegated to playing the center position. The front office had to make a move for Timofey Mozgov to cover the defensive mistakes that Love was committing. The coaches would even give more minutes to Tristan Thompson off the bench because of his skills at the defensive end. In the 2015 playoffs, when Love was injured, many people began to think that Cleveland was better off without him as Thompson's defensive energy fueled them to an appearance in the NBA Finals.

However, one cannot put all the blame on Kevin Love for those shortcomings. As said, nobody can blame him for playing behind LeBron James. However, Love his one of the best power forwards down at the low post. This means that you can always rely on him to score inside when he gets the ball to a spot. However, he was relegated to playing the role of a stretch power forward to widen driving lanes for LeBron James and Kyrie Irving. One indication of such is the fact that Love has attempted half of the free throws per game he's attempted in his best years in the Timberwolves. That means he gets fewer touches to get opportunities to fish fouls inside the paint.

Had the coaches made use of Kevin Love's ability to create shots inside the paint, his numbers wouldn't have dipped. He surely would have still been a perennial All-Star with numbers that jump up the roof. Nevertheless, the Cleveland Cavaliers' are LeBron James' team, and coaches will always do what's necessary to make life easier for their best player on the floor. Apparently, what makes life easier for LeBron to win games in Cleveland is for Love to stretch the floor to open up driving lanes. And the Cavs are winning. Love would never trade wins for good numbers. He had good numbers in Minnesota, but he was losing.

Superstar statistics are useless in the greater scheme of winning games and even possibly a championship.

Chapter 7: Love's Legacy and Future

Kevin Love is a unique NBA talent. As a scorer, he's as complete of an offensive package as you can get. Kevin Love is a great player down at the low post. At 6'10" and 250 pounds, Love bullies smaller players inside the paint. If up against players of the same size, his superior footwork and his wide range of post moves allow him to score against any defense. There are a lot of power forwards with the same offensive talents inside the paint. What makes Love more unique than any of those guys is the fact that he could shoot the three-pointer at such a high level. He's an excellent spot-up shooter that could also use that part of his game to get defenders off-balanced for easy driving lanes to the basket.

Again, there are also players that have that combination of inside and outside scoring abilities. You can mention Dirk Nowitzki, whose inside and perimeter scoring skills are probably second to none in the history of the NBA. You could also mention Chris Bosh and LaMarcus Aldridge as guys with the same kind of offensive talents. However, what makes Kevin Love stand apart from those big men is the fact that he rebounds at such a high rate that you wouldn't even think he camps out on the perimeter for about 50% of the offensive plays. That's uncommon considering that perimeter players find it difficult to get excellent positioning inside the paint for offensive rebounds. That's just simply a testament to how great a rebounder Kevin Love is.

In addition to all of his offensive talents, Kevin Love is a great passer for a big man. He's always been considered an excellent passer since his college days in UCLA. When he's outside the three-point line or when he's on the high post, expect Love to find teammates whenever he's not in the position to put up points himself. A lot of NBA big men have that skill. You can mention guys like Kevin Garnett, Joakim Noah, the Gasol brothers, Blake Griffin, and Draymond Green as big men that could make plays for other teammates. However, what makes Love unique among those players is his ability to make long outlet passes, a skill of his which is considered almost second to none. When he gets defensive rebounds, expect his teammates to run as hard as they could to the other end of the floor in the hopes of getting accurate long passes from Kevin Love. He is simply a man with unique skills. That's why a lot of analysts were excited of pairing him with LeBron and Kyrie. Imagine Love collecting a rebound and suddenly throws an outlet pass to a streaking LeBron James or Kyrie Irving for an easy basket.

No other NBA player comes to mind when talking about Love's combination of inside-outside scoring abilities and rebounding prowess. The only player that comes close is Charles Barkley. Charles shot a lot of perimeter jumpers while claiming tons of rebounds in his prime years. He's also a terrific passer at the power forward spot. However, at about 6'4", Barkley did not have the size to get as many baskets in the low post as Kevin Love does. He could not post up other NBA big men because of his size disadvantage. The only time he scores at the blow block is when he's matched up with smaller players. In contrast, Love was always a great player down at the block. That's why no other NBA player comes close in comparison to Love's talents.

Because of his skills, Kevin Love developed to become the Minnesota Timberwolves' lone superstar and designated franchise player after Kevin Garnett left to go to Boston. While it is a certainty that Garnett is the best player to have ever played in Minnesota, Love's place behind KG is not far behind because of his talents of putting up points on the board and grabbing tons of rebounds. With the numbers he put up for the Timberwolves, it is arguable that he is the franchise's second best player next to Kevin Garnett.

Kevin Love is the Minnesota Timberwolves' third all-time leading scorer. With 6,989 total points in Minnesota, he is third behind Sam Mitchell's 7,161. However, it took Mitchell 10 seasons in Minnesota to do it whereas Love needed only six. Love is also the Timberwolves' second all-time leading rebounder at 3,108 total boards. The only guy who lords over him in total rebounds is Kevin Garnett, who has 8,130 rebounds collected as a Timberwolf. Regarding other all-time statistics, no other Minnesota player can contend with Love for the franchise's spot as the second-best player in team history. One can argue that the Minnesota Timberwolves' short history and lack of great players are the reasons why Love figures so high on top of the franchise's all-time stats. However, you can never disregard Love's penchant for putting up points and grabbing rebounds when he was in Minnesota.

While Love has struggled to win for years as a member of the Timberwolves, the future now looks brighter, but also tougher than ever. The trio of LeBron James, Kyrie Irving, and Love are among the favorites to win an NBA championship for more seasons to come, but perhaps none of the three faces more pressure than Love. If the Cavaliers should fail, LeBron can fall back on the fact that he has already won two championships with the Miami Heat, while Kyrie Irving can excuse himself by his relative youth and the fact that he is not viewed as a superstar in the same way which Love and LeBron are. He also lacks as much playoff experience as Kevin Love does. Love will have such no excuse. Just as LeBron once faced incredible pressure to win his first championship, Love must now prove his ability to win.

However, with how the Cleveland Cavaliers have been giving more emphasis on both LeBron James and Kyrie

Irving, nobody could blame Kevin Love for his lack of contributions on both the scoring and on the rebounding end of the floor for the Cavs. A lot of people have been saying for two years that the Cleveland coaches have been underutilizing Love's offensive gifts. Love is one of the best power forwards when it comes to scoring inside the paint and outside the three-point line. Almost no other big man in the league has his offensive skill set. Yet, he is primarily used as a stretch power forward in Cleveland. That has hurt his scoring numbers a lot as he was left to shooting low-percentage shots from the outside. Even his rebounding numbers dropped because he couldn't get offensive rebounds.

Despite that, the Cleveland Cavaliers have made the NBA Finals in 2015 and are now the top team in the Eastern Conference. The reason for that is primarily because of LeBron James' brilliance in spite of Kyrie's inexperience and of Love's lack of production. They also have good role players such as Mo Williams, Richard Jefferson, JR Smith, Iman Shumpert, Tristan Thompson, and Timofey Mozgov. Hence, though Love's numbers may have been hurt in his two years with the Cavs, everything is alright as the team is winning games. Kevin Love was never a selfish athlete. He's not one to trade wins for superstar numbers.

Whether Love will finally get a ring in Cleveland is yet to be decided. We might not even know if he will spend the rest of his career as a Cavalier because of how he is sorely underutilized in Cleveland. All we know is the fact that Kevin Love is playing hard to the best that he could and that he is playing according to what is needed from him by the coaches to get wins. With the way he's being used as a stretch power forward in Cleveland, we might not even see him playing in the All-Star Game ever again. However, a player of Love's talents and unselfishness will always take years of contending for an NBA title than empty All-Star selections.

Final Word/About the Author

I was born and raised in Norwalk, Connecticut. Growing up, I could often be found spending many nights watching basketball, soccer, and football matches with my father in the family living room. I love sports and everything that sports can embody. I believe that sports are one of most genuine forms of competition, heart, and determination. I write my works to learn more about influential athletes in the hopes that from my writing, you the reader can walk away inspired to put in an equal if not greater amount of hard work and perseverance to pursue your goals. If you enjoyed *Kevin Love: The Inspiring Story of One of Basketball's Dominant Power Forwards,* please leave a review! Also, you can read more of my works on *Colin Kaepernick, Aaron Rodgers, Peyton Manning, Tom Brady, Russell Wilson, Michael Jordan, LeBron James, Kyrie Irving, Klay Thompson, Stephen Curry, Kevin Durant, Russell Westbrook, Anthony Davis, Chris Paul, Blake Griffin, Kobe Bryant, Joakim Noah, Scottie Pippen, Carmelo Anthony, Grant Hill, Tracy McGrady, Vince Carter, Patrick Ewing, Karl Malone, Tony Parker, Allen*

Iverson, Hakeem Olajuwon, Reggie Miller, Michael Carter-Williams, John Wall, James Harden, Tim Duncan, Steve Nash, Pau Gasol, Marc Gasol, Jimmy Butler, Dirk Nowitzki, Draymond Green, Pete Maravich, Kawhi Leonard, Dwyane Wade, Ray Allen and Paul George in the Kindle Store. If you love basketball, check out my website at claytongeoffreys.com to join my exclusive list where I let you know about my latest books and give you lots of goodies.

Like what you read? Please leave a review!

I write because I love sharing the stories of influential people like Kevin Love with fantastic readers like you. My readers inspire me to write more so please do not hesitate to let me know what you thought by leaving a review! If you love books on life, basketball, or productivity, check out my website at claytongeoffreys.com to join my exclusive list where I let you know about my latest books. Aside from being the first to hear about my latest releases, you can also download a free copy of *33 Life Lessons: Success Principles, Career Advice & Habits of Successful People*. See you there!

Clayton

Made in the USA
Middletown, DE
20 January 2021